ultra sports

ultra swimming

by Claudia B. Manley

the rosen publishing group's
rosen
central

Published in 2002 by The Rosen Publishing Group, Inc.
29 East 21st Street, New York, NY 10010

Library of Congress Cataloging-in-Publication Data

Manley, Claudia B.
Ultra swimming / by Claudia B. Manley.— 1st ed.
p. cm. — (Ultra sports)
Includes bibliographical references and index.
Summary: Introduces ultra or long-distance swimming, exploring such key elements as training, safety, gear, and competition and profiling ultra swimmers, past and present.
ISBN 0-8239-3558-2 (lib. bdg.)
1. Long distance swimming—Juvenile literature. [1. Long distance swimming. 2. Swimming. 3. Swimmers.] I. Title. II. Series.
GV838.53.L65 M36 2001
797.2'1—dc21

2001003352

Manufactured in the United States of America

Contents

19.95

Introduction: Maximum Distance

How far can you push your body? It seems like the more technology makes our daily lives easier, the more we crave greater challenges. Endurance sports have become increasingly popular over the past ten years. These events and activities are designed to challenge the individual athlete. Marathons and triathlons, as well as adventure races like the Eco-Challenge and the Raid Gauloises, all cater to individuals seeking to push the limits of their bodies and minds.

What are ultra sports? When we talk about ultra sports, or in the case of this book, we're talking about sports that are very intense and focused versions of activities many of us do for fun. For example, let's say you like to swim, and when you swim you often do ten or fifteen laps in a pool.

Ultra swimming takes place in open water, such as a lake or an ocean, rather than the controlled confines of a pool.

To become an ultra swimmer, you would need to leave the pool behind, jump into a lake or an ocean, and tackle many miles.

Ultra swimming is long-distance swimming, outside the confines of a pool. Because it takes place in lakes and oceans, it is also referred to as open-water swimming. For ultra swimmers, the term "long distance" can refer to a swim consisting of one mile or over one hundred miles. When you're an ultra swimmer, it's often just you and miles and miles of ocean.

Ultra swimming appeals to people who like to break out beyond the bounds of the pool. With no ropes to keep you in your lane or walls from which to push off, swimming becomes an ultra challenge. Not surprisingly, to be an ultra swimmer you have to be in the very best shape.

Ultra swimming also appeals to those athletes who like to have an element of chance thrown into their swim. Sure, an ultra swimmer can chart the tides and check the weather, but once he or she is out in a large lake or fickle ocean waters, anything can happen. In addition to ever changing environmental factors, an ultra swimmer has to contend with predatory fish (like sharks), boats, and the anxiety that can result from swimming in a seemingly endless ocean.

People of all ages take to swimming the oceans of the world. For instance, Gertrude Ederle was only nineteen when she became the first woman to swim the English Channel. Because it is low-impact, swimming is also great exercise for seniors. Many swimmers continue to swim well into their eighties and nineties.

Ultra swimmers of all ages should become knowledgeable about safety, training, nutrition, and equipment. We'll explore the world of ultra swimming and provide you with information to consider if you think ultra swimming is the sport for you. Remember, once you get out of the pool and into the open water, it's a whole new game.

So how long have people been diving into the ocean? Well, there is archaeological evidence that people swam as early as 2500 BC. While we don't know the distances, it is likely that they swam in local bodies of water.

The Romans were the first to build swimming pools. They even created a heated one in the first century BC. Not surprisingly, the earliest known swimmers hailed from Rome, Egypt, Greece, and Assyria.

Throughout the Middle Ages, Europeans shied away from swimming; this was due in part to a backlash against bathing. At that time, many people believed that illnesses spread in still waters. They feared that swimming or bathing in water with others would leave them open to disease. As a result, the first formal swimming organization in Europe wasn't formed until 1837. Founded in London, England, the club met at any of the city's six indoor pools.

Many ancient Romans (depicted here) enjoyed the benefits of bathing and swimming.

One of the earliest open-water clubs, the Brighton Swimming Club, was founded in England in 1860. At that time, open-water bathers fought vigorously to keep from getting knocked down by the sea waves. This gave a local group of tradespeople interested in promoting the positive effects of bathing and swimming an idea. They decided to invite swimmers to gather on the local beach. They also encouraged more experienced swimmers to teach other people to swim. The club went on to host races and encourage others to swim as well. It is still in existence today.

As is the case with other ultra sports, endurance events began to garner more attention over time. The English Channel, considered by

Gertrude Ederle

Gertrude Ederle is one of the greatest American figures in the history of swimming. Not only was she the first woman to successfully swim the English Channel, but she also broke the existing men's record, too! Born in New York City in 1906, Ederle was a competitive swimmer at an early age.

Between 1921 and 1925, she held twenty-nine national and world amateur swimming records. At the 1924 Summer Olympics in Paris, France, she won a gold medal in the 400-meter freestyle relay and bronze medals in the 100-meter and 400-meter freestyle races. She was also a leading eight-beat crawl (eight kicks for each full arm stroke) swimmer.

Her ability and competitiveness led her to consider tackling one of the greatest challenges of her day: swimming across the English Channel. At that time, only five men had successfully crossed the channel. Some people thought that women were incapable of accomplishing this feat, but Ederle was set on proving them wrong.

In 1925, she made her first attempt, but she was unsuccessful. Not deterred by this setback, Ederle, at age nineteen went back to France the following year. On August 6, 1926, she left the shores of France and began the thirty-five-mile swim toward England. Ederle arrived on the shores of Dover, England, fourteen hours and thirty-nine minutes later, beating the men's world record by nearly two hours!

Following her success, she toured as a professional swimmer until a back injury kept her out of the water for many years. She later returned to swimming as an instructor, teaching deaf children. In fact, the channel crossing had permanently damaged her hearing. She was inducted into the Swimming Hall of Fame in 1965 and the Women's Sports Hall of Fame in 1980.

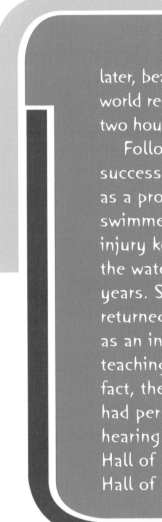

Gertrude Ederle

many to be the Mount Everest of open water, presented the greatest challenge to modern swimmers. For many years, it was considered impossible to swim because of the treacherous conditions.

Many factors make swimming the channel difficult. The English Channel is 19 nautical miles long (1 nautical mile equals 1.1508 land miles or 1,852 meters), and for years it has served as the main trade and travel connection between the British Isles and continental Europe. This means a lot of boat traffic. It's like a water highway.

Extremely strong tides that change direction every six hours further complicate channel swims. This, combined with unpredictable weather (most forecasts are only approximations and can change very quickly), makes the sea very rough. The success rate for solo swims, even today, is only 50 percent. The first man to successfully swim across the English Channel was Captain Matthew Webb. On August 24, 1875, he slipped into the channel and reached the shores of France in twenty-one hours and forty-five minutes.

While Webb's crossing definitely made headlines, people remained reluctant to take to the open water for organized swims of any length. In 1909, the Fédération Internationale de Natation Amateur, roughly translated as the International Amateur Swimming Federation, was founded. This organization, commonly referred to as FINA, is the governing body of open-water championships. Not only does it sanction traditional length swims, it also oversees a series of marathon swimming events.

Ultra Swimming Today

Illustrating the current interest and ever growing popularity of long-distance swimming, in 2001, FINA scheduled eleven meets on three continents. The 2001 series of races started on February 4 in Argentina (Santa Fe-Coronda). The competition also included Egypt, the first African country ever to participate in the FINA Marathon Swimming World Cup.

These days there are more and more opportunities for ultra swimmers to test their endurance and skill. Some current organized

This Manhattan Island Swim contestant tackles the Hudson River during the annual twenty-eight-mile race around Manhattan, New York on June 12, 1999.

events are the Manhattan Island Swim (28 miles around the island of Manhattan), the Tampa Bay Marathon Swim (24 miles), and the Lake Saint-Jean International Swimming Marathon in Quebec (32 kilometers, or 19.8 miles).

Other ultra swimmers might like the challenge of the Chesapeake Bay Swim. This is a 4.4-mile event that follows the span of the Chesapeake Bay Bridge in Maryland. It is held in early June when the water temperature is between 64 and 72 degrees Fahrenheit. Temperatures generally range from 53 degrees Fahrenheit to 78 degrees Fahrenheit. Of course, if you're taking a quick dip during the winter, you can expect colder temperatures. A good way to test whether you should use a wet suit is to submerge your hand for ten seconds. If you can barely stand it, wear a wet suit. Also, you might consider a wet suit if you've gotten into the water and after a minute or so of light swimming, your skin is chilled or your limbs feel like they are going numb.

If you're headed to warmer climates, the Victor 12.5-mile swim around Key West, Florida, is a swim around the island of Key West. Held in early June, the water temperature is a nice 82 degrees. The St. Croix Coral Reef Swim is a 5-mile swim from Buck Island to St. Croix located in the U.S. Virgin Islands. It is held yearly in the first weekend of November. Water temperatures around that time average 77 degrees.

One of the oldest open-water swims in the United States is the Boston Light Swim, a 10-mile swim held during the third week of August. The race runs from the Boston Harbor Islands to the L Street beach. Water temperatures range from 53 to 68 degrees.

United States Masters Swimming

United States Masters Swimming (USMS) is an organization of swimmers ranging in age from 19 to 100. The organization offers open-water swimming clinics. These clinics provide swimmers with a hands-on opportunity to experience and explore open-water swimming. Veteran swimmers explain technique, navigation, pacing, safety, nutrition, and more. Some clinics also include USMS-sanctioned open-water races and events.

If you are interested in learning more about ultra swimming, becoming involved in an organized group event is a great idea. In general, participating in an organized group swim can give you the security that independent solo swims lack. The association sponsoring the race should ensure that there are officials on hand. They will also be prepared to respond to almost any emergency. There are opportunities to become involved in group races the world over. Ultra swimming events take place in South Africa, France, Australia, Germany, Portugal, Brazil, Egypt, and the United Kingdom. Check out the resources section in the back of this book for more information on these events and others.

If you are considering becoming an ultra swimmer, you should already be a strong swimmer. Just as no one would ever suggest competing in a marathon to the first-time runner, no one should learn to swim by crossing the English Channel. If you are already a pretty serious swimmer, there are some training techniques that can help prepare you for the open water. You will need to make time to train in many ways: in the water, on land, and in your mind. Combining these three elements can prepare you to undertake one of the greatest swimming challenges around: ultra swimming.

In the Pool

Initially, you should train in a pool. Inside and outside of the pool, though, start thinking of distance in terms of quarter, half, and whole miles instead of meters or laps. Open-water swims typically do not use these metric markers. The shortest open-water races are usually around a mile long (triathlons and mini-triathlons may have shorter swims). A mile is just the tip of the iceberg. A serious ultra swimmer looks forward to a twelve-mile swim across his or her local lake.

The pool is an optimal place to practice bilateral breathing (breathing while turning your head in either direction). Bilateral breathing is very important because when wind and water slap one side of your face, you can turn your head, face the opposite direction, and breathe more comfortably. Breathing also helps keep you relaxed and composed during your swim. Developing this breathing technique while in the pool is essential to achieving success in open water. You should also practice raising your head to look forward two to three times per lap. This will enable you to spot landmarks, give you a sense of location, and help you swim in the right direction.

Generally, your in-pool workouts should vary. In addition to going for maximum distance, you should also mix in some speed intervals to increase your overall speed. To do this,

Although ultra swimming takes place in the open water, it is wise to do your initial training in a pool.

Ultra swimmers need to incorporate some weight training into their routines.

alternate measured sprints with recovery periods that allow your heart rate and breathing to go down to normal. For example, sprint the length of the pool and then do an easy lap to recover. Guides to complete workouts can be found in some of the resources in the back of this book. If you're currently on a swim team, you can talk with your coach about your desire to try ultra swimming. He or she can also help you set up an individualized workout.

Working on your endurance in terms of both time and distance is essential to meeting the ultra challenge. In addition to increasing the distance you swim, also practice swimming for a set time. Often you'll find that during a given period you may not have swam as far as you thought you might. Swimming in the open water takes more time and effort than it does in the pool.

On land, focus on your cardiovascular (heart and lung) conditioning, muscular or strength conditioning, and flexibility. Any exercise that raises heart rate and keeps it raised for at least twenty minutes benefits your cardiovascular system. You want to make sure you get that kind of workout at least three times a week. Incorporating running, cycling, or in-line skating into your regimen will strengthen your heart and lungs, so you can keep swimming mile after mile.

A weight-training workout builds up key muscles, like those in your shoulders, arms, back, and abdomen, as well as your legs. Strong parts contribute to a strong whole. Strength training should be done at least three times a week. While you weight train, remember to pay attention to your posture and breathing. Make sure you work your muscles smoothly, using a full range of motion.

Finally, keeping your muscles flexible will help prevent cramps. Priming your muscles this way also helps keep you from injuring unprepared or tight muscles. A stretching program or regular yoga classes are great for increasing flexibility. Overall cross training adds variety to your routine and keeps you from becoming bored.

The Mental Edge

One of the biggest challenges for a swimmer new to the open water is maintaining composure. That means not panicking in the middle of a long swim. Panicking can be very dangerous and in extreme cases can lead to drowning accidents. If you start to freak

Cardiovascular exercises, such as running, give the ultra swimmer the endurance required to swim long distances.

out a little in open water, just take a moment to relax—tread water, float on your back for a few minutes, or switch to an easier stroke.

Some ultra swimmers listen to music before a long swim. Then, they replay the music in their heads as they peel off mile after mile. It can become a form of meditation.

Visualization is also a great tool to use before and during a swim. One of the benefits of visualization is that you can slow down, repeat, or even stop the action in your head. Take a moment to visualize yourself in the water and watch your strokes. If you've been having difficulty maintaining proper body position, correct it in your mind. Eventually, your body will follow your mind's lead. Visualization can also help calm an anxious mind. Imagining how it will feel when you have reached your goal can be both exhilarating and reassuring.

Recovery

Sometimes the desire to train hard and progress quickly can cause you to overdo it. Many athletes use the term "overreaching" to describe stress that results from excessive training. Symptoms of this are fatigue, loss of technique (getting sloppy), lessening of swimming economy (it takes more effort to work out), and unusual aches and pains in joints and muscles.

One way to recover from this is to combine active and passive activities. This means that instead of just sitting out and chillin' on the boardwalk, you continue to work out, but differently. Combining nonswimming activities with more active training gives your body a break and keeps you in shape.

Passive recovery doesn't mean that you're doing nothing. You want to do something that is relaxing but still invigorating.

Bowling can be a refreshing part of passive recovery.

Think about a massage, alternating hot whirlpool baths with a brief dip in a cold pool, resting with your legs raised, or even participating in a group activity like bowling.

The idea is to continue to stimulate your metabolism. Metabolism refers to the chemical reaction that takes place in each of your cells. This reaction is what changes nutrients in the food you eat into energy. The faster your metabolism is, the quicker you'll get energy from your food.

While your active recovery shouldn't wear you out, it should involve all your muscles. Again, cross training is a great way to actively recover. You shouldn't try to perform these activities with the same level of intensity that you put into your swimming workouts. Instead, stagger your heavy-duty and more leisurely workouts. This not only helps keep your muscles strong but also helps you stay psychologically attached to working out.

Taking time to recover from overreaching or injury is important. Continuing to push through, especially if you often feel awful, will ultimately be counterproductive. If you burn out quickly because of chronic fatigue or repeated injury, you will never know what it really feels like to push your limits and come out of a swim feeling like a different person.

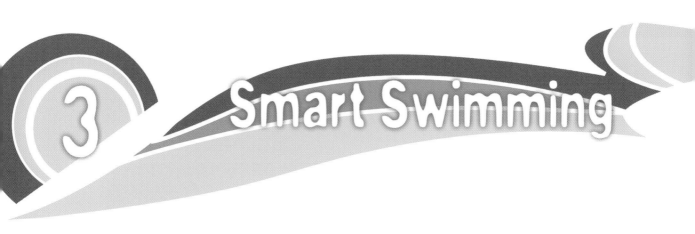

It is important to consider and prepare for the risks and potential dangers involved in any new sporting activity. For instance, when you ride a bike, you should wear a helmet to prevent head trauma should you fall. Race car drivers use seat belts, helmets, and padding to protect themselves. While swimmers don't use the same kind of protective gear, they can protect themselves in several ways. Proper nutrition, training, knowledge of water safety, and learning about a racecourse in advance of a long swim are all essential elements of staying safe.

Gearing Up for Your First Race

As you begin to train as an ultra swimmer, start small. As you grow stronger, you can increase distance. Practice swimming at least one mile, both in a pool and in open water. When you feel ready, try competing in a one-mile race. The relatively short distance and the presence of race officials and trained support crews will help ensure that you stay safe. This will also provide you with an excellent opportunity to try out new skills. Once you get the feel of it, you can advance to longer group events and perhaps train for more extensive solo swims.

Nutrition and Energy

As an athlete in training, your first priority is to supply your body with energy. An easy way to determine how many calories the average person should consume is to multiply his or her weight in pounds by twelve. But as an ultra athlete you need a lot more! The average endurance athlete can consume 25 calories per pound of body weight. So while a nonathletic person who weighs 125 pounds might need to consume 1,500 calories per day, an endurance athlete of the same weight would want to consume 3,125 calories per day.

Today, many different approaches to sports nutrition are popular. Some people recommend eating a diet that is high in protein and low in carbohydrates (carbs). Others believe that eating foods rich in carbohydrates and low in fat is the way to go.

Endurance athletes typically benefit from a diet high in carbo-hydrates. Some athletes devote 75 percent of their daily diet to carbohydrate-rich foods such as pasta, breads, fruits, and vegetables. Bodily carbohydrate reserves drop during intense workouts. Getting tired and running out of energy, also known as bonking, is often the result of this loss of carbohydrates. As an ultra athlete, you need to make sure you have enough fuel to push your body through often long and grueling training sessions or races.

As a budding ultra athlete, you should make sure that 15 percent of your diet consists of protein. Protein helps rebuild muscle and repair tissue. It provides long-term energy as well as vitamins and minerals. Protein can come from animal sources, such as meat, cheese, and fish, or nonanimal sources, such as tofu and other soy products.

Despite all the negative hype concerning fat, it is an important element of any diet. In proper doses, fat can help sustain your energy level. Make sure you go for high-quality fats like those found in olive oil, avocados, and nuts rather than animal fats and saturated fats found in fast food. Fat should make up about 15 to 25 percent of your diet.

A diet high in carbohydrates gives the ultra swimmer the energy needed to endure long races.

Timing Is Everything

Don't forget to pay attention to the timing of your meals. Many athletes find that eating many small meals, rather than three large ones each day, is the most effective way to maintain a high energy level. You should plan to eat a meal high in carbs about three to four hours before training. If you decide to have a little snack, have it fifteen to thirty minutes before your workout. Try yogurt, toast with jam, or bananas.

It is important to keep your body's fuel tank full. You can destroy your muscles if you train without having eaten enough food. We all know what happens when a car runs out of gas. If that happens to you in open water, it could spell serious trouble. Before training, avoid high-fiber and high-fat foods. They can cause gas and slow down digestion. In this way, they also divert energy you need for your swim.

Water, Water Everywhere

Even though as an ultra swimmer you are constantly in water, it is very important to remain hydrated. That means drinking plenty of water throughout the day. Sports drinks serve to hydrate your body as well as help replace electrolytes and provide carbohydrates. Dehydration is a serious threat and has caused many ultra swimmers to head for the shore. If you are attempting to swim a superlong distance, your support team should provide you with water and sports drinks. If you're preparing for a shorter training swim, have a sports drink before you hit the water and make sure you drink up when you get back to land.

After a swim, remember to eat carbs in order to replenish the reserves you just depleted. This is the best time for your muscles to

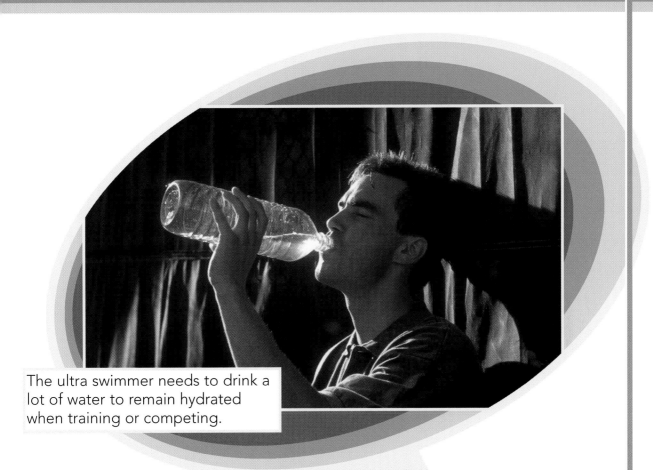

The ultra swimmer needs to drink a lot of water to remain hydrated when training or competing.

restore the energy that you just used. Ideally, you should eat within twenty minutes after training, but if you eat within two hours, you should still benefit from this refueling. Carbohydrates such as bagels, bread, rice cakes, and raisins are good. Including some protein, like tuna fish or peanut butter, also helps aid muscle and tissue repair at this time.

Safety First

When you start training in open water, it is critical to keep safety in mind at all times. When you leave the controlled environment of a pool and swim in open water, you will encounter many constantly varying conditions. Planning ahead for some open-water conditions is crucial. Don't let your enthusiasm override your common sense; start training in open water gradually. Begin with shorter swims and build up to the long ones.

Start out swimming close to the shore in shallow water. That way, if you tire more quickly than you had anticipated, you won't have to go far to rest. Swimming in shallow water also gives you a chance to become familiar with the tides and currents in relative safety. The tide changes each day according to the position of the earth in relation to the sun and the moon. Tides are a change in the level of the sea or ocean due to changes in the earth's gravitational force. Currents are the result of gravity, wind friction, and water density variations in the various parts of the ocean. A current is defined as the vertical and horizontal circulation of the ocean water.

When you start training in open water, do not attempt to swim the same distance or for the same length of time as you do in a pool. In open water, you should start with five minutes of swimming. That may not sound like much of a swim, but as you're not used to volatile open waters, you may find that you tire much more easily. As you become stronger and more comfortable in open water, you can add minutes to your time. This will also ultimately translate into longer distances.

Never swim alone. Someone should always be close by in case something goes wrong and you need help. You might also think about swimming in open water with an experienced swimmer. If you can't find someone who can swim with you, try to have someone follow you in a kayak or canoe, or at least have someone watch you from shore. If you're swimming on a guarded beach, inform the lifeguard that you are a long-distance swimmer in training. A support team is crucial to a longer swim. A support team can consist of just one person following

The ultra swimmer must be prepared to face the ever changing conditions of the open water.

you in a kayak to make sure you don't get into trouble, or a boat carrying a doctor, trainer, the captain, and family members.

Be aware of boat traffic. Boats are like cars to a runner. Often the boats don't see a swimmer until it's too late. Try to swim away from popular boating areas. If that's not possible, wear an orange-colored swim cap. Orange is the universal color of warning.

Remember to use sunscreen. It's easy to forget, but the reflective property of water (meaning sunlight will bounce off the water and onto you), combined with time spent exposed to the sun, can lead to a nasty sunburn at the very least. With prolonged sun exposure, you also risk skin cancer.

Solo Swims of Ontario

On September 7, 1974, seventeen-year-old Neil MacNeil became separated from his pace swimmer (someone who swam alongside him to keep him from going too fast or too slow) and the boat carrying his support team while attempting to swim from Youngstown, New York, to Toronto, Ontario. He disappeared and was presumed drowned. Solo Swims of Ontario (SSO) is a nonprofit organization that was founded in 1975 in response to this fatal accident.

First and foremost a safety organization, SSO is sponsored by the government of Canada and run by volunteers. It governs individuals who are interested in long-distance solo swims in the province of Ontario. It monitors solo swims in the Great Lakes, including Lakes Ontario, Erie, and Huron. The average cross-lake distance of Lake Ontario is thirty miles. Anyone considering a long-distance solo swim in Lake Ontario must have the swim sanctioned by SSO.

One of its chief concerns is that swimmers follow safety guidelines. SSO provides advice during all stages of planning a solo swim. It also sponsors safe and successful long-distance swims as a means of encouraging ultra swimming.

Anyone considering a solo swim is assigned a

representative, the swim master, who accompanies the swimmer on his or her swim to make sure all safety guidelines are met. In addition to being an experienced long-distance swimmer, the swim master also knows boat safety, cardiopulmonary resuscitation (CPR), first aid, and other rescue techniques. The swim master oversees a swimmer's mandatory ten-mile trial swim. This test verifies that a swimmer is physically fit and prepared for an ultra swim.

SSO also provides each potential solo swimmer with an information kit containing a checklist of necessary items and equipment. It provides some boat safety essentials, like chemical glow-lights to be worn by the swimmer after dark. Ultimately, SSO helps a swimmer meet the challenge of "beating the lake," making sure that each swimmer is mentally and physically prepared to go the distance.

If you're out for a long swim, try to fuel up every fifteen minutes. Stop and have a sports drink or energy bar. But don't hang out with your support team (either on the kayak or on the boat) snacking for too long. The cold water will start to take away your body heat and your muscles will become stiff.

Should you experience cramping, try to release a cramp in your calves by turning your toes toward your knees. This will stretch those muscles. If you have cramps in other areas, float on your stomach while massaging the problem area. Obviously, there's a lot to consider before you head out for that long swim. Training and proper planning can help you return safely to shore.

You might think that the only gear an ultra swimmer needs is a swimsuit, but there are other products that can enhance the safety and performance of an ultra swimmer. Goggles are definitely important. They'll help protect your eyes from the stinging salt of ocean waters or irritants in freshwater lakes. Using smoke-tinted or mirrored goggles can also help cut down glare from the sun. A swim cap will not only help keep you warm but will protect your hair from the drying effects of salt water (or chlorine) and the sun.

Fins

Many ultra swimmers use fins. Used as a training aid, they can improve ankle flexibility, improve kick strength, and help establish proper

Ben Lecomte

Ben Lecomte accomplished what many had thought impossible: swimming across the Atlantic Ocean! And not only did he succeed, he also used it as an opportunity to raise money for cancer research. His father's death from cancer prompted this heroic trek.

Lecomte spent eight years training for the swim from Hyannis, Massachusetts, to Quiberon, France. Not only did he swim six days a week, but his regimen also included cross-training activities like cycling and calisthenics.

On July 16, 1998, he began his swim, hoping to complete the ocean crossing in eighty days. He chose that time of year because the weather is best in the Atlantic Ocean from May through September. Leaving Hyannis in July gave Lecomte plenty of time to swim in good weather.

Although the weather was good, the water in the Atlantic was still very cold, so Lecomte wore a wet suit. He also used fins to help propel him through the water. His average speed was two knots per hour (roughly 2.24 miles per hour).

He swam at least six hours a day with a shark POD. The shark POD is a protective ocean device that looks sort of like a large plastic bubble. It protects the swimmer by emitting an electronic field to keep away sharks and other dangerous ocean creatures. It's like a force field for the swimmer.

When he wasn't swimming, he drifted with the currents and winds on a boat. The boat's skipper and one crewmember constituted his support team. Together they kept an eye on weather conditions and made sure that their route took advantage of currents going eastward, toward France.

Ben Lecomte celebrates with his girlfriend, Trinh Dang, after his cross-Atlantic swim in 1998.

Lecomte also planned ahead, bringing plenty of food to eat. It was very important that he consumed enough calories each day to help him stay strong in the water. During his swim, he consumed between 7,000 and 8,000 calories a day.

On September 25, 1998, seventy-two days after he began his journey, he reached Quiberon, France. He swam a total of 3,736 nautical miles!

Many ultra swimmers use fins to help them train.

body position. They also help increase swimming speed. Some swimmers wear them during their solo swims or during group competitions. As some competitions do not allow swimmers to use fins, find out the rules and regulations regarding gear before race day.

There are several different kinds of fins. Short-bladed fins do not add much speed, but they help give your kick an extra boost. Medium-bladed fins add even more power but reduce the speed of your kick. The change in power and speed is due to the increased surface area of the fins. Single-bladed fins, also known as monofins, are great for strengthening leg, abdominal, and back muscles. In fact, these fins are so popular that some competitive events are devoted to swimming with monofins.

Flotation Devices

Another item on the market that can help ultra swimmers stay safe is an inflatable flotation device. Even experienced, strong swimmers can find themselves overcome by difficult water conditions, cramps, or strong currents. Should a swimmer get into trouble because of a muscle cramp, fatigue, or adverse weather conditions, a flotation device enables him or her to remain afloat until help arrives.

The Hydro Belt is one such device. It is designed so that it has no buoyancy when it's deflated and therefore doesn't interfere with swimming. If a swimmer experiences trouble, he or she can inflate it with just the pull of a cord. While flotation belts can prove helpful, it is important to remember that no Coast Guard standards exist for inflatable flotation belts. (There are no official guidelines for how they should perform or how they are made.) They should never be used as a substitute for a support team.

As we've already mentioned, you should always have a support person or team on hand during long, solo swims. Your support team should also have proper medical training. They don't have to be doctors, but they should know how to care for you until a doctor arrives.

Hypothermia

The right gear can also reduce the possibility of hypothermia, one of the potential dangers involved in ultra swimming. Hypothermia is an abnormally low body temperature. As normal body temperature is 98.6 degrees Fahrenheit, hypothermia is serious at any temperature below 95 degrees. Hypothermia necessitates emergency treatment when body temperature drops to 90 degrees.

Ultra swimmers have to watch out for hypothermia because of the extended time they spend in the open water. Water conducts (acts as a transporter for) heat faster than air, so loss of body heat occurs even more rapidly in cold water. Hypothermia can reduce cellular activity of body tissue, slow the heart rate, and cause unconsciousness. Because pulse and respiration slow and blood pressure is depressed, hypothermia victims can appear to be dead. This condition is called a hypothermic coma.

Wearing a wet suit is one way in which a swimmer can combat hypothermia.

Reviving a victim of hypothermia involves the slow and gradual rewarming of his or her body. Using blankets and other indirect applications of heat is important because if the increase in body temperature exceeds more than one or two degrees Fahrenheit per hour, the cardiovascular system can collapse. With proper treatment, the survival rate of people in a hypothermic coma is close to 75 percent.

To help protect against hypothermia, wear two swim caps instead of one. Up to 30 percent of your body heat can escape from your head. This is one way to keep yourself warm.

Some swimmers also coat lamb's wool with Vaseline and stick it in their ears to reduce body heat loss. If you are going to be in cold water for a long time and you are not wearing a wet suit, coat your body with lanolin (a wool-based grease). This will help keep your body warm.

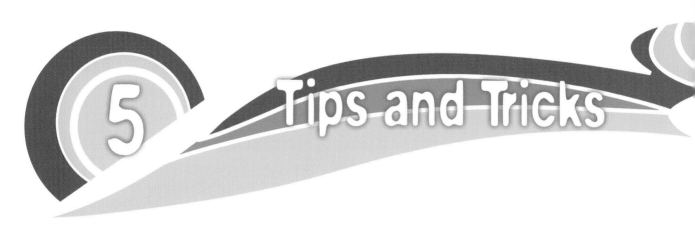
Knowing handy tips, tricks, and techniques can help you achieve the optimum training or racing experience! As a novice ultra swimmer, you may not be used to the extreme cold temperatures of some open waters. Cold water can cause you to gasp. Don't panic! Just relax and try to breathe deeply. If possible, splash some water on your arms or over your entire body before your swim. This will help your body and mind acclimate to the water temperature.

Stretches

Stretching before and after your swims is a treat for your muscles and a terrific way to prevent injury.

Hyperextension stretch:
   Stand with your back straight. Bring your arms up behind your body. Hold and repeat.

Rotation stretch:
   Stand with your back straight. Stretch your left arm out straight in front of you and rotate it clockwise ten times. Reverse the direction and then switch arms.

Tricep stretch:
   Stand with your back straight. Bring one arm up and back with the elbow bent behind your head. Take the opposite arm and gently apply pressure to intensify the stretch. Repeat with the other side.

Hamstring stretch:
   Sit on the floor with your right leg extended and your left leg bent so that your knee is next to your chest. Slowly begin to slide the bent leg down; you'll feel a stretch in the back of your right leg. When you feel an easy stretch, hold the position for twenty seconds.

Don't round your lower back; try to keep it straight. Slide your leg back up to release. Switch sides and repeat.

Note: Repeat each of these stretches eight to ten times, holding each stretch for a few seconds.

It can also be difficult to exhale when your face is in the cold water, but you need to continue breathing. During your training swims, remember to breathe out forcefully. With practice, it will become easier for you to jump right into awesome form come race day.

Speaking of race day, a great way to speed up your swim time is a special technique for cornering buoys (floating objects anchored at specific locations to guide swimmers). Race organizers often use buoys as mile markers or to indicate a turnaround point in a race. As you approach the buoy, turn on your back. Continue to roll over onto your stomach and then pivot 90 degrees, cradling the buoy with your body. This will sharpen the angle of your turn and keep you from adding unnecessary time and distance to your swim.

Practice pacing yourself. As you train for distance, figure out how long you can sustain a certain pace. Adding interval training (alternating short and fast swimming with long and slow periods) will help add speed to your pace. When you plunge into a competitive swim, maintain an even pace. Conserving a bit of energy during a race will enable you to turn it on at the very end and to sprint to the finish.

Hair and Skin Care

The extensive time spent in pools or open water can take its toll on your hair and skin. Both chlorine and salt water dry them out. Wearing a swim cap helps protect your hair from these elements. Some swimmers also put conditioner in their hair before putting their caps on, also known as "cap and condition." If you decide to cap and condition before swimming in a pool, make sure that your cap fits snugly. This will prevent the conditioner from leaking into the pool.

After your swim, wash your hair thoroughly. Because elements like chlorine can penetrate the hair shaft, just rinsing your hair off won't do the trick. You'll also probably want to deep condition your hair once a month. Some swimmers avoid hair concerns altogether, opting to shave their heads.

In addition to using sunscreen to protect your skin, you should also moisturize it after training. Despite the fact that you've spent all that time in the water, your skin will be dehydrated. Rehydrating your skin after training keeps it supple and prevents cracked and peeling skin. Taking care of both body and mind will keep you in ultra form.

Some swimmers shave their heads to avoid damaging their hair.

Ultra swimmers participate in two types of events: solo swims and group swims. Solo swims involve the solitary struggle of the individual swimmer against choppy lake or ocean waters. Group swims, however, add a whole new dimension to competition. In addition to a grueling swim, you also have to deal with your fellow swimmers.

Group Competition

By the time you participate in an organized competition, you will have devoted many hours to training, both in the water and on land. You have trained not only your body but also your mind. Hopefully, you have learned

Ultra swimmers run into the water to get their bodies used to the water temperature.

how to handle some of the mental games—doubt, anxiety, panic—that may go on in your head while you are in the water for long periods of time.

Competing actually starts the day before the event. Check out the course. If there are buoys set up, count them. This will help you figure out where you are during the race.

In order to familiarize yourself with water temperature and currents, practice running from shore into the water. When the water reaches the middle of your thigh, dive in. This practice will help your entry into the water on race day feel more natural.

Susie Maroney

Australian Susie Maroney is an ultra, ultra swimmer. Throughout the 1990s, she set new swimming records in both distance and time. In 1996, she became the first person to successfully swim the 112-mile length of the Florida Straits from Cuba to the United States. And this was right after completing a 90-mile swim through shark-infested waters from Jamaica to Cuba.

She had attempted the Florida Straits swim in 1995 but was forced to stop just twelve miles from the finish because she was dehydrated and fell ill. She had been in the water for thirty-eight hours! Maybe the reminder of that painful journey was what gave her the speed and strength to complete the swim in 1996 in just over twenty-four hours.

While her swim might have been fast, it was anything but easy. Strong winds and currents almost forced her to quit again. She suffered multiple jellyfish stings as well as sunburn, and her tongue was swollen from the salt water. Her support team included two boats, one that towed the cage in which she swam (to protect her from sharks). The cage was battered during her swim but not enough to stop her. The other support vessel included a navigator, her doctor, and friends and family.

Maroney started swimming at age three to help her asthma. Initially, she was not a strong swimmer. She developed her swimming skills over time. A native of Australia, she considers Cuba her second home.

Maroney has also crossed the English Channel twice. She also broke her own record for the most distance covered in twenty-four hours. She'd originally set it at fifty-eight miles; getting from Cuba to Florida was almost twice that distance!

Susie Maroney

On the day of the competition, do some kind of warm-up exercises to get the blood flowing and your heart rate up. Jogging in place is good, as are jumping jacks. These aerobic activities will also help take the edge off any prerace jitters that you might be experiencing. Do some stretches as well. Keeping your muscles flexible is very important.

More than 2,000 athletes jump into the water at the start of a race in Nice, France, on June 18, 2000.

And They're Off!

When the starter's gun goes off, take your time. If you're worried about running into other competitors, stay back. That way, you'll also be less likely to encounter them in the water. Find your space. Some swimmers think that it's better to start in front, but that's only if you're a very strong swimmer who can keep up the winning pace. Swim behind and at the edge of the pack. There, you can carve out room to swim. If your body tangles with someone's elbow or foot, don't panic. It is only a bump in your road to the finish. Think of it as a temporary break in your physical stride and mental concentration.

Some ultra swimmers prefer to race against time and the rigors of open waters instead of against other competitors.

Be prepared to adjust your stroke according to water conditions. Feel the swells and go with them. If the water is choppy, a high elbow recovery (your elbow should be high above your head as you follow through your stroke) is important. Going under, rather than through, large waves will help you to maintain your pace.

If a number of competitors surround you, try drafting. Drafting is when you swim closely behind another swimmer. The swimmer in front of you creates a path of less water resistance for you. In fact, this technique can help you save 20 to 30 percent of your energy.

Perhaps one of the most important things to remember during competition is to have fun. You're swimming because you love it! If you're not having fun during a race, then why are you competing? Take some time to appreciate your surroundings and you'll find it easier to get into the zone.

Are You an Ultra Swimmer?

Are you picturing yourself out there in water right now? Can you see your strong strokes overcoming the waves of the ocean? Maybe you're ready to train for your own ultra swim.

People swim for fun and for fitness. Ultra swimming adds a challenge to the sport and can be a rewarding way to exercise your body and mind for many years. United States Masters Swimming groups sponsor marathon events for adult swimmers ranging in age from 19 to 100!

Before undertaking ultra swimming, you should seriously consider the training and safety issues presented here. Again, swimming in open water for long distances can prove risky. Ultra swimming can be a great way to test your physical and mental limits, but it should always be done safely.

Should you become serious about this sport, there are a number of opportunities not only to compete but also to teach and train others. The increasing popularity of the sport brings with it a demand for experienced swimmers to show budding distance swimmers the ropes. Coaching others is a rewarding way to invite new swimmers into the sport and extend its appeal.

After all, the earth is made up primarily of water. A world full of aquatic challenges awaits you. Dive in!

Glossary

anxiety Uneasiness of mind; fear.

calisthenics Exercises performed without special equipment.

carbohydrate Compound composed of carbon, hydrogen, and oxygen that serves as an energy source (pastas and breads are common sources).

cardiovascular Relating to the heart and blood vessels.

chronic Having a long duration or frequent recurrence.

composure Calmness of mind.

current Movement of a lake or ocean that is independent of the tides.

electrolyte Substance that moves electric currents in the body in positively and negatively charged particles (ions); in sports drinks it is usually salt that acts as an electrolyte.

emit Throw or give off.

fatigue Tiredness.

hypothermia Abnormally low body temperature.

metabolism Chemical changes in the body that help produce energy.

muscle Tissue whose function is to produce motion.

passive Not using a lot of energy.

predatory Relating to the killing or destroying of another animal or person.

protein Highly complex substance directly involved in the chemical processes essential for life (high concentrations are in meat, eggs, milk, and beans).

sanction To give approval.

tide Change in the level of the sea or ocean due to changes in the gravitational force relative to the position of the earth to the moon and sun.

tissue Structurally and functionally similar cells and intercellular material.

Ultra Info

Aqua Moon Adventures
P.O. Box 9448
Coral Springs, FL 33075
(954) 755-3318
(800) 356-5132
e-mail: info@randynutt.com
Web site: http://randynutt.com/aqua9.html

Boston Light Swim
63 Van Winkle Street
Dorchester, MA 02124
(617) 474-2400
e-mail: johnwerner@citizenschools.org

Catalina Channel Swimming Federation
P.O. Box 1358
Cambria, CA 93428
(805) 927-0604
e-mail: swimcatalina@earthlink.net
Web site: http://www.swimcatalina.org

Fédération Internationale de Natation
Avenue de l'Avant-Poste 4

1005 Lausanne, Switzerland
+41 21 310 4710
Web site: http://www.fina.org

Manhattan Island Foundation
P.O. Box 959
Ansonia Station
New York, NY 10023
(888) NYC-SWIM (692-7946)
(212) 873-8311
e-mail: info@nycswim.org
Web site: http://www.nycswim.org

24 Mile Tampa Bay Marathon Swim
Distance Matters, Inc.
1920 Cobblestone Way
Clearwater, FL 33760
(727) 531-7999
(888) 524-7803
e-mail: president@distancematters
Web site: http://distancematters.com/marathon

United States Masters Swimming
National Office
P.O. Box 185
Londonderry, NH 03053-0185
(603) 537-0203
(800) 550-SWIM (7946)
e-mail: usms@usms.org
Web site: http://www.usms.org

In Canada

Masters Swimming Canada
MSC National Office
P.O. Box 3365
Meaford, ON N4L 1A5
(519) 538-5548
e-mail: bethmsc@bmts.com
Web site: http://www.compusmart.ab.ca/masterssc

Swimming/Natation Canada
National Office
2197 Riverside Drive, Suite 700
Ottawa, ON K1H 7X3
(613) 260-1348
e-mail: natloffice@swimming.ca
Web site: http://www.swimming.ca

Web Sites

About Swimming
www.swimming.about.com

Ben Lecomte's trip across the Atlantic—Cross Atlantic Swimming Challenge
www.swimatlantic.com

Channel Swimming & Piloting Federation (CS&PF)
www.channelswimming.net

Channel Swimming Association
www.channelswimmingassociation.ltd.uk

Chesapeake Bay Swim
www.bayswim.com

Irish Long Distance Swimming Association
www.ildsa.com

Open Water Marathon Swimming (great site for international information)
www.oceanswims.com

The Swim Ring
www.k-swimming.org/swim-ring

Camps for Kids

Advanced Swim Team Program
203 Golden Hind
Corte Madera, CA 94925
(800) 227-6629
(415) 927-7800
e-mail: team@somaxsports.com
Web site: http://www.somaxsports.com/swimteamprogram.htm

Fluid Mechanics Swim Camp
P.O. Box 343
Middletown, NJ 07748-0343
(800) 266-5179
(732) 957-9787
e-mail: swim@fluidmechanics.net
Web site: http://www.fluidmechanics.net

Girl Power Swim Clinics
200 Merry Hill Drive
Raleigh, NC 27606
e-mail: premier@usaswimmer.com
Web site: http://www.usaswimmer.com

Nike Swim Camps—US Sports Camp
919 Sir Francis Drake Boulevard
Kentfield, CA 94904
(415) 459-0459
(800) NIKE CAMP (645-3226)
e-mail: swim@ussportscamps.com
Web site: http://www.ussportscamps.com

Total Immersion Swimming
171 Main Street
New Paltz, NY 12561
(800) 609-7946
(845) 256-9770
e-mail: info@totalimmersion.net
Web site: http://www.totalimmersion.net

YMCA/YWCA
101 North Wacker Drive
Chicago, IL 60606
(312) 977-0031
(888) 333-YMCA (9622)
Web site: http://www.ymca.net

Ultra Reading

Books

Brems, Marianne. *Swimming—Going for Strength and Stamina.* Chicago, IL: Contemporary Books, 1988.

Dean, Penny Lee. *Open Water Swimming.* Champaign, IL: Human Kinetics, 1998.

Laughlin, Terry, with John Delves. *Total Immersion: The Revolutionary Way to Swim Better, Faster, and Easier.* New York: Fireside, 1996.

Sleamaker, Rob, and Ray Browning. *Serious Training for Endurance Athletes.* 2nd ed. Champaign, IL: Human Kinetics, 1996.

Watson, Kathy. *The Crossing: The Extraordinary Story of the First Man to Swim the English Channel.* New York: J.P. Tarcher/Putnam, 2001.

Wennerberg, Conrad. *Wind, Waves, and Sunburn.* South Brunswick, NJ: Breakaway Books, 1997.

Whitten, Phillip. *The Complete Book of Swimming.* New York: Random House, 1994.

Publications

Swimmer
P.O. Box 7421
Red Oak, IA 51591
(800) 846-0086
Web site: http://www.swimmeronline.com

SwimNews
356 Sumach Street
Toronto, ON M4X 1V4
(416) 963-5599
(888) 328-0490
Web site: http://www.swimnews.com

Total Swim
Web site: http://www.totalimmersion.net/articles.html

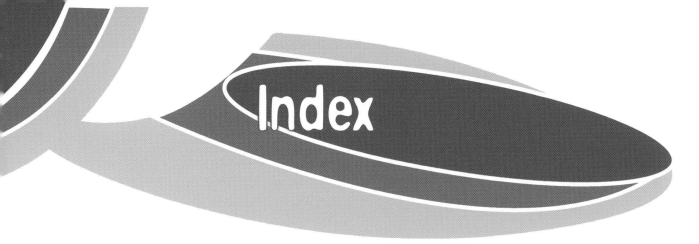

Index

tips and tricks for, 40–43
training for, 16–22

T

Tampa Bay Marathon Swim, 14
tides, 28
training, 16–22
  in a pool, 16–19
triathlons, 5, 17

U

ultra swimming
  beginning, 24, 28
  defined, 5–6
  events, 12, 14
  with groups, 15, 44–50
  and hypothermia, 38

support teams for, 29–30, 37
tips and tricks for, 40–43
training for, 16–22
USMS (United States Masters
  Swimming), 15, 50

V

visualization, 20

W

warming up, 47
water, drinking, 26
water temperature, 14, 37–38, 40, 45
Webb, Captain Matthew, 12
weight training, 19
wet suit, 14, 39
women swimmers, 10–11, 46–47

Credits

About the Author

Claudia B. Manley is a writer living in Brooklyn, New York, with her son, her partner, and their cat, Max.

Photo Credits

Layout and Design

Thomas Forget